The Wit
of Robert Burns

The humour of Burns: in his sunny moods a full, buoyant flood of mirth rolls through his mind. – Thomas Carlyle

Robert Burns — Man of Wit

The Wit
of Robert Burns

Compiled by
Gordon Irving

LESLIE FREWIN of LONDON

Also by Gordon Irving

Great Scot! (The Harry Lauder biography)

The Wit of the Scots

The Devil on Wheels

The Story of Annie Laurie

The Solway Smugglers

First published 1972 by
Leslie Frewin Publishers Limited,
Five Goodwin's Court,
Saint Martin's Lane, London, WC2N 4LL, England

This book is set in Bembo
Printed and bound in Great Britain by
R. J. Acford Limited,
Industrial Estate, Chichester, Sussex, England

World Rights Reserved
ISBN 0 85632 048 X

This book of Robert Burns' wit and wisdom is dedicated to the many millions, in many lands, who, despite the diversions of a space and television age, still find time to honour the memory of a peasant poet and his home-spun wit and humour.

CONTENTS

Introduction

Was Robert Burns, poet, philosopher and man-of-letters, a man of wit as well?

There are some who will say he wasn't, maintaining that he was too serious in purpose, too genuine in emotion, to have the time or taste for wit and humour. Certainly, the serious side of Robert Burns is evident throughout his writings.

But *The Wit of Robert Burns* can be proved conclusively many times, as close students of his works know.

Burns had a short and unhappy life, albeit a full one, but his tragic moments were fortified by his ability to laugh at life and people, and to aim a shrewd and witty barb at persons who deserved it.

In fact, the gifts of humour and wit often saved him from despair and kept him going in bad times. They helped to create the fun and frolic in his brief but full life.

The witty side of Burns is best summed up, I think, by his biographer, J. G. Lockhart, who wrote of him: 'He was the standing marvel of the place; his toasts, his jokes, his epigrams, his songs, were the daily food of conversations and scandals.'

According to Lockhart, a most reliable chronicler, Burns was a companion in wit much sought after. From castle to cottage every door flew open at his approach.

'If,' said Lockhart, 'he entered an inn at midnight, after all the inmates were in bed, the news of his arrival circulated from the cellar to the garret; and 'ere ten minutes had elapsed, the landlord and all his guests were assembled round the ingle . . .

'The stateliest gentry of the county, whenever they had special merriment in view, called in the wit and eloquence of Burns to enliven their carousals.'

In the stately old homes of Scotland the wit of Burns made the great ladies smile, and the attractiveness of his personality endeared him to all.

All over Scotland, and further afield, another side of his nature, the 'wicked wit' of Burns, as it was once described, was also well known. This was the Burns who waxed witty about *poseurs*, humbug, false appearances, dandies and fops; the Burns who hated name-droppers and sycophants. He made many such into figures of ridicule through the use of a choice phrase or rhyme.

Nevertheless, I can't fully agree with Robert Heron, his first biographer, who describes the wit of Burns as being a sort of wicked wit, and suggests that it outrages all the canons of good taste and moral propriety.

'Wicked' his wit may be – in certain places, especially where he feels strongly against a hypocrite or a *poseur*, but the epithet can hardly be ascribed generally to his writings. There is, on the other hand, much of a kindly vein running through a goodly quota of his humour.

Each January about 500,000 Burns suppers are consumed by gatherings numbering from four to over 1,000 admirers, and in scores of countries. That estimate is by the Burns Federation, to which some 350 clubs are affiliated. Philadelphia alone has 18,000 members, and there are clubs all over Australia and Canada.

The wit of Burns is appreciated by many millions of people from Moscow (where there are Burns enthusiasts and students galore, and where his memory is revered) to Mauchline, in Ayrshire, a village he knew so well.

He is honoured at lavish banquets in New York and Montreal and Melbourne and London. Exiled Scots gather to recite his lines and analyse his character, from South Africa to New Zealand, from British Columbia to Oklahoma.

At the same time, worthy Scots, keeping up a tradition, drink to his memory at modest Burns Suppers by the hundred in the tiny village halls of the Highlands and Lowlands.

Robert Burns was wittiest, I am convinced, in what he wrote and spoke about women, whose virtues and foibles he knew so well. He had a close knowledge as well as a practical adoration of the female sex, and he could epitomise their faults as well as their virtues in telling and memorable lines.

That is why, in this book, I have been able to devote a separate section to Burns and his wit about the bonnie lasses-O.

The ploughman poet is surely proved a true humorist and man of wit because he remained, in both his good times and bad, a man of such tolerant good humour. The student knows that, where Burns at any point loses patience, it is nearly always with those who have no humour in their hearts.

A recent news-agency despatch told the world that African schoolboys are now learning *Tam O'Shanter* for their English O-Level exams. Burns himself would have been the first to see the amusing side of such an item. His wit is human and gentle, even if some of it is also 'wicked'. As a man of the people, reared in hard times and circumstances, he had to laugh at life; being a man-of-wit helped him through many a misfortune.

Bardowie Loch, Scotland   Gordon Irving

For A' That!

Robert Burns, humble countryman that he was, disliked to be tutored in matters of taste, and hated all kinds of idolatry.

Once, visiting a fine house with a group of people and admiring beautiful objects, he was asked by a lady at his side: 'But, Mr Burns, have you nothing to say of this?'

To which, glancing at the leader of the party, he replied:

Nothing, madam, nothing, for an ass is already braying over it!

*   *   *

The poet was holding forth in the King's Arms Inn at Dumfries, and discussing the death of a fellow-townsman whose funeral was to take place the following day. 'I wish you would lend me your black coat for the occasion,' said a friend. 'My own is in need of repair.' Burns replied that he would be attending the funeral himself, and would therefore be unable to lend him his coat. He added:

But I can recommend the most excellent substitute. Throw your character over your shoulders. That will be the blackest coat you ever wore in your lifetime.

*   *   *

Burns was handed a letter by a literary friend, Dr Blair. It suggested that he take time and leisure to improve his talents, adding: 'For on any second production you give to the world, your fate, as a poet, will very much depend.'

Burns laughed, pushed the letter into his pocket, replying:

Thank you, Doctor; but whiles a man's first book, like his first bairn, is the best.

*   *   *

The poet happened to be standing on the quay at Greenock one day when a rich merchant from the town suddenly fell into the harbour. A sailor dived in and rescued him. The merchant put his hand in his pocket and gave the sailor a shilling. When the watching crowd protested at the smallness of the sum, Burns told them to stop their protests, and added, quietly:

This gentleman is himself the best judge of the value of his own life.

*   *   *

Burns went to a church service at Lamington, in Lanarkshire, and found the place cold and uncomfortable, the weather chilly, and the sermon extremely poor. He left these lines on the pew:

> As cauld a wind as ever blew,
>   A caulder kirk, and in't but few;
> As cauld a preacher's ever spak'
>   Ye'll a' be het* ere I come back.

* hot, or roasted in Hell!

*   *   *

The poet saw Jean Armour, his future wife, for the first time one day in Mauchline, Ayrshire. Jean was seventeen, and was spreading clothes on a bleach-green along with some other girls, when Burns passed by.

With him was a little dog, which ran on top of the clothes. Jean Armour scolded and threw a stick at the animal, whereupon Burns replied:

Lassie, if ye thought ocht o' me, ye wadna' hunt my dog.

*   *   *

One day Burns was walking along a village street, adopting his customary pose of keeping his eyes on the ground, deep in thought, when he suddenly met the two Misses Biggar, daughters of the parish minister.

One of the young ladies called his name and then reprimanded him gently on his lack of attention to the fair sex. Instead of looking towards the ground, she said, he should be indulging in the 'most priceless privilege of man,' that of beholding and conversing with the ladies.

Robert Burns listened quietly, then replied:

Madam, it is a natural and right thing for man to contemplate the ground from whence he was taken, and for woman to look upon and observe man, from whom she was taken!

*   *   *

Burns was visiting a well-known beauty spot, Creehope-Linn, in Dumfriesshire, and at every turn of the stream and bend of the wood, he was called upon loudly to admire the scene.

Finally, tiring of criticism that he did not show rapture enough, he stopped and said:

But I could not admire it more, gentlemen, if He who made it were to ask me to do it.

*   *   *

Visiting Moffat, in Dumfriesshire, with a musician friend, Burns called for a bumper of brandy. 'Oh, not a bumper,' said the musician. 'I prefer two small glasses.'

Burns replied:

Two glasses? Why, you are just like the lass in Kyle who said she would rather be kissed twice, bare-headed, than once with her bonnet on.

*   *   *

At a dinner party Burns was talking to Mrs Montague about his children, and particularly of his eldest son, whom he called a promising boy. He added the comment:

And yet, you know, madam, I hope he will turn out a glorious blockhead, and so make his fortune!

*   *   *

The quiet wit and humour of Burns the poet is seen in these rarely-quoted lines:

>   Good Lord, what is man; for as simple he looks,
>   Do but try to develop his hooks and his crooks,
>   With his depths and his shallows,
>   His good and his evil,
>   All in all, he's a problem must puzzle the devil.

*   *   *

A certain peeress sent an invitation to Burns to attend at her home, but had not sufficiently cultivated his acquaintance before-hand.

  At the time an animal known as 'The Learned Pig' was being exhibited for entertainment in the Grassmarket of Edinburgh.

  When Burns received the lady's invitation, he sat down and wrote this reply:

Mr Burns will do himself the honour of waiting on Her Ladyship provided she will invite also the 'Learned Pig'.

*   *   *

Burns was nevertheless fond of praise and liked sincere flattery, especially when it came from the lips of an accomplished lady. He once replied to Mrs McMurdo:

Madam, your praise has ballooned me up to Parnassus.

*   *   *

The poet called one day at his printer's in Kilmarnock, and produced his poem The Holy Fair. *Asked if he was not afraid to launch such an attack on the clergy, he replied:*

As to my purse, you know they can make nothing of it. As for my person (brandishing his oak stick), I carry an excellent cudgel!

*   *   *

Despite his great triumph as a poet in Edinburgh, Burns returned to the simple life of an Ayrshire farmer, saying:

I'll be damned if I ever write for money.

*   *   *

On literature generally, Burns had this to say:

Some books are lies frae end to end.

*   *   *

Burns visited a rich gentleman's library and was shown a fine collection of books. Unfortunately, the owner was not fully able to appreciate the contents and revealed more than a little ignorance about the writings:

He told Burns, before he left, that he was particularly anxious about the bindings of his books.

Next morning the owner found these lines, left by Burns on his library table:

> Through and through th' inspir'd leaves
>   Ye maggots, make your windings;
> But O, respect his lordship's taste,
>   And spare the golden bindings.

*   *   *

Touring the Western Highlands of Scotland, the poet called at an inn at Inveraray, and found the inn-keeper more eager to serve the guests of the Duke of Argyll than to look after the traveller Burns. Next day he departed, leaving these lines:

> Whoe'er he be that sojourns here,
>   I pity much his case,
> Unless he comes to wait upon
>   The Lord their God, 'His Grace'.

*   *   *

Burns brought a sense of gentle humour and wit even to his letter-of-the-law duties as an Exciseman.

One moonlight night he was awakened by the clatter of galloping horses, looked out of the window, and noted it was smugglers.

'I fear ye'll be to follow them, then,' said his wife, Jean.

Burns replied:

And so I would, Jean, were it Will Gunnion or Edgar Wright; but it's poor Brandyburn, and he has a wife an' three weans, and he's no' doin' verra weel in his farm. What can I do?

*   *   *

In the Dumfriesshire village of Thornhill a poor woman named Kate Watson had taken up the publican's trade without a licence.

Robert Burns, the Exciseman, entered her home, summoned the poor Kate to him, and, slyly pointing to her contraband goods, remarked:

Kate, wumman, are ye mad? Don't you know the Supervisor and I will be upon you in the course of forty minutes? Goodbye t'ye for the present!

*   *   *

Burns' sense of charm and wit is seen in this apology he made for failing to correspond with a friend:

If you can, in your mind, form an idea of indolence, dissipation, hurry, cares, change of country, entering on untried scenes of life, all combined, you will save me the trouble of a blushing apology.

*   *   *

The poet was asked if the scholarly people he had met in Edinburgh had helped to improve his poems by their criticism. He replied:

Sir, these gentlemen remind me of some spinsters in my country, who spin their thread so fine that it is neither fit for weft nor woof.

*   *   *

Quotation from Burns:

> I hae naething to lend –
> I'll borrow frae naebody.

*   *   *

Robert Burns, on a tour of Scotland, visited the Carron ironworks area and was refused admittance to the works.

   Noting the resemblance between the huge flames leaping into the sky from the furnaces and the Presbyterian conception of Hell, he came out with these lines:

> We cam na here to view your works,
> In hopes to be mair wise,
> But only, lest we gang to Hell,
>   It may be nae surprise;
> But when we tirl'd at your door
>   Your porter dought na hear us,
> Sae may, shou'd we to Hell's yetts come,
>   Your billy Satan sair us!

*   *   *

Burns, in a letter to Mr Josiah Walker, at Blair of Athole, Dunkeld, said:

I shall ever be happy to send you the cogitations of my mind, the occurrencies of my life, or the productions of my Muse; on condition that you just pay me, as I said before, *in kind*.

* * *

The poet thus described one of his acquaintances:

A wit in folly, and a fool in wit.

* * *

Robert Burns felt that a practical knowledge of life and the world was the best of all lessons:

Education is no substitute for Common Sense.

* * *

Burns had a happy outlook on his own profession as a poet, as shown when he wrote:

> I am nae poet, in a sense,
> But just a rhymer like by chance;
> An' hae to learning nae pretence;
> Yet, what the matter?
> Whene'er my Muse does on me glance,
> I jingle at her.

* * *

In expressing love he also had a witty and happy turn of phrase, as shown by his verse about 'My Nanie, O', otherwise Agnes (Nanie) Fleming, a servant girl in the employment of his friend Gavin Hamilton.
  Of her, Burns wrote:

Come weel, come woe, I care na', but
   I'll tak what Heav'n will sen' me, O;
Nae ither care in life have I,
   But live, an' love my Nanie, O.

*   *   *

*Was Burns the very first perfervid Scottish Nationalist? Or is
this merely an instance of his impish, mischievous humour?*

   *He made a journey on horseback over the Border into England,
along with his friend, Robert Ainslie, W.S. They arrived at
Coldstream where the River Tweed divides England from
Scotland.*

   *Mr Ainslie suggested that they should cross the river by the
bridge, so that Burns could boast that 'he had been in England.'*

   *They did so, and were walking slowly along on English
territory when Burns suddenly tossed off his hat, and with bared
head, knelt down, lifted his hands, looked towards the other side
of the Tweed and Scotland, and began to recite from his poem*
The Cottar's Saturday Night –

O Scotia! my dear, my native soil!
For whom my warmest wish to Heaven is sent.

*   *   *

*There was a touch of wit even in Robert Burns' very first rhyme
which he wrote after recalling a childhood incident when one
evening, at family worship, a rat came down from the rafters to
the floor by means of a rope which his mother was using to hang
up the day's washing.*

   The young wit-in-the-making observed:

A rat, a rat, for want of stairs,
Ran down a rope to say its prayers.

*   *   *

Burns, the awkward soldier, served as a volunteer at Mauchline, in Ayrshire, and on one occasion, when the corps was being exercised in firing, he made more than one bad discharge.

The captain, angry, asked: 'Is this your erratic genius, Mr Burns, that is spoiling your fire?'

To which the poet-soldier replied:

No, it can't be me, Captain, for look ye – I have forgot my flint.

*　　*　　*

The Lasses-O!

Burns – and, of course, rightly so – considered himself an expert on the ladies and the lasses, their virtues and their foibles. He sampled a fair number of them in his short life, and came to know them intimately.

The extent of his penetrating wit about women is seen to advantage in some of his many comments on the fairer sex:

One evening Burns was invited to Lord Monboddo's house in Edinburgh, and, among the gentry present, met his host's beautiful daughter, Miss Burnet.

On his return, a friend asked him: 'Did you admire the young lady?

To which Burns replied:

I admired God Almighty more than ever. Miss Burnet is the loveliest of all His works.

*   *   *

The poet made this plea in verse:

> Oh, gi'e me the lass that has acres o' charm,
> Oh, gi'e me the lass wi' the well-stockit farms!

*   *   *

Burns was the super-flatterer of all time, particularly in reference to the ladies:

> Auld Nature swears, the lovely dears
> Her noblest work she classes, O;
> Her 'prentice han' she try'd on man,
> An' then she made the lasses, O.

* * *

In an Epistle to Dr Blacklock:

A wife's head is immaterial compared with her heart.

* * *

To Clarinda, Mrs Agnes McLehose, Burns wrote:

Your thoughts on religion, Clarinda, shall be welcome. You may perhaps distrust me when I say 'tis also my favourite topic, but mine is the religion of the bosom.

* * *

In his poem Green Grow the Rashes, *Burns sums up his obvious pleasure at being among the ladies:*

> But gi'e me a canny hour at e'en,
> My arms about my dearie, O;
> An' war'ly cares, an' war'ly men
> May a' gae tapsalteerie, O.

* * *

Robert Burns was attending church in Dumfries. Sitting in the pew in front of him was a young lady, a certain Miss Ainslie. The text of the sermon was a 'fierce denunciation of obstinate sinners.'

The poet, always with an eye to helping the ladies, noticed the young girl frantically thumbing through the pages of her Bible for the text. Scribbling a verse hurriedly, he handed it to her:

Fair Maid, you need not take the hint,
　　Nor idle texts pursue;
'Twas guilty sinners that he meant,
　　Not angels – such as you!

*　　　*　　　*

Writing about gossip among women, Burns said:

The Ladies arm-in-arm in clusters,
　　As great an' gracious a' as sisters;
But hear their absent thoughts o' ither,
　　They're a' run deils an' jads thegither.

*　　　*　　　*

Burns wrote not only of Miss Ainslie but of all sweet women when he said:

She unites three qualities rarely to be found together: keen, solid penetration; sly, witty observation of remark; and the gentlest, most unaffected female modesty.

*　　　*　　　*

To his lady-friend Clarinda, the poet once posed this question:
Why are your sex called the tender sex, when I never have met with one who can repay me in passion?

*　　　*　　　*

Burns could be gentle and flattering on the subject of women, but he could also be scathing at times, as in this earthy description of Willie Wastle's wife:

25

> She has an e'e – she has but ane,
>   The cat has twa the very colour;
> Five rusty teeth, furbye a stump,
>   A clapper-tongue wad deave a miller;
> A whiskin' beard about her mou',
>   Her nose and chin they threaten ither –
> Sic a wife as Willie has
>   I wadna gie a button for her.

*   *   *

In Tam O'Shanter, *quoted all round the world, Burns offers these simple lines of witty comment on wifely relations:*

> Ah, gentle dames! It gars me greet
>   To think how mony counsels sweet,
> How mony lengthen'd sage advices,
>   The husband frae the wife despises.

*   *   *

In 1780 Robert Burns and his friends formed a literary and debating society in a little 17th-century house in the village of Tarbolton, in Ayrshire. One of the objects was deep philosophical debate – but the rules of the club demanded that all members be 'confessed lovers of the ladies'.

With more than a touch of irony, for which Burns himself must have been largely responsible, they called themselves:

'THE BACHELORS' CLUB!'

*   *   *

More wise thoughts about the weaker sex, all from Burns:
Who would not be in raptures with a woman that will make him £300 the richer?

*   *   *

If ye gi'e a woman a' her will,
Gude faith! She'll soon o'er-gang* ye.
(* . . . over-ride you)

*　　　*　　　*

Ev'n silly women have defensive arts,
Their eyes, their tongues – and nameless other parts.

*　　　*　　　*

Dear deluding woman,
The joy of joys.

*　　　*　　　*

What signifies the life o' man,
　　An' 't were na for the lasses, O!

*　　　*　　　*

A man may kiss a bonnie lass,
　　An' aye be welcome back again.

*　　　*　　　*

When awful Beauty joins with all her charms,
　　Who is so rash as rise in rebel arms?

*　　　*　　　*

*In an unusual (but surely not to be taken seriously!) comment
on women, Burns offers this line in* The Inventory;
I ha'e nae wife, and that my bliss is!

*　　　*　　　*

The poet was always very conscious of the way women change their ideas:

> Tho' women's minds, like winter winds,
> May shift and turn, and a' that!

*   *   *

In his Epitaph on a Henpecked Squire, *Burns wrote:*

> Here lyes a man a woman rul'd,
> The devil rul'd the woman.

*   *   *

And, in another reference to a brow-beaten husband, he says:

> Curs'd be the man, the poorest wretch in life,
> The crouching vassal to a tyrant wife.

*   *   *

> Let us mind, faint heart ne'er wan
> A lady fair.

*   *   *

In his well-known poem Comin' Thro' The Rye, *Burns comments on the thrill of secret courtship:*

> Gin (if) a body kiss a body,
> Need a body tell?

*   *   *

The poet's all-embracing fondness of women is shown in this philosophy:

> The one sacred Right of Woman is . . . protection.

*   *   *

Robert Burns, on the contrariness of the gentler sex:

> Ladies arm-in-arm in clusters,
>> As great and gracious a' as sisters,
> But hear their absent thoughts o' ither:
>> They're a' run deils and jads thegither.*

(* jad=giddy young girl; a'run deils=downright devils)

* * *

The value of a husband listening to his wife, as exemplified in Tam O'Shanter:

> O Tam, hadst thou but been sae wise,
> As ta'en thy ain wife Kate's advice.

* * *

In a letter, dated 13 June 1780, to Mrs Dunlop at Haddington, Burns wrote:

The most placid good nature and sweetness of disposition; a warm heart, gratefully devoted with all its powers to love one; vigorous health and sprightly cheerfulness, set off to the best advantage by a more than common handsome figure: these, I think, in a woman, may make a tolerable good wife, though she should never have read a page but 'The Scriptures of the Old & New Testament,' nor have danced in a brighter Assembly than a Penny-pay Wedding.

* * *

Burns, a connoisseur, had many a native turn of wit on the subject of women – girls, ladies, Mesdames, the lasses, call them what you will! One whom he often visited went as a young married woman to settle at Goldielea, near Dumfries, Maria Woodley, daughter of the Governor of the Leeward Islands.

When Lord Buchan asserted in public that women ought always to be flattered grossly, or not spoken to at all (!), Burns, with due gallantry, addressed these lines to the lovely Maria:

> Praise Woman still! His Lordship says,
>   Deserved or not, no matter;
> But thee, Maria, when I praise,
>   There Flattery cannot flatter.

*   *   *

Burns, reflecting on his personal good fortune in having the bonnie and homely Jean Armour for a wife, wrote, in July 1788:

Circumstanced as I am, I could never have got a female Partner for life who could have entered into my favourite studies, relished my favourite authors, etc., without entailing on me, at the same time, expensive living, fantastic caprice, apish affectation, with all the other blessed, Boarding-school acquirements, which . . . are sometimes to be found among females of the upper ranks, but almost universally pervade the Misses of the Would-be gentry.'

*   *   *

On Love

Love is a very special word with Robert Burns, and occurs throughout his writings. This is only to be expected from such a self-confessed admirer of the ladies and bonnie lasses.

Some of the poet's wittiest moments come when he speaks or writes on the subject of romance.

In one of many letters to friends, Burns explains how romance inspired him to his chosen career:

I never had the least thought or inclination of turning poet till I once got heartily in love. Then rhyme and song were the spontaneous language of my heart.

*   *   *

About the perils of loving over-much, Burns says:

> Had we never loved sae kindly,
> Had we never loved sae blindly,
> Never met – or never parted –
> We had ne'er been broken-hearted.

*   *   *

The poet's fondness at an early age for romance is seen in this excerpt from his writings:

I felt as much pleasure in being in the secret of half the loves of the parish of Tarbolton as ever did statesman in knowing the intrigues of half the courts of Europe.

*   *   *

In Duncan Gray, *he writes:*

Slighted love is sair* to bide.
(* . . . is hard to endure)

*   *   *

Burns believed sincerely that a man must have practical experience of what he wrote about. On love and the business of writing about love, he said:

I have often thought no man can be a proper critic of love composition except he himself, in one or more instances, has been a warm votary of this passion.

*   *   *

More lines of wit from Robert Burns on the internationally popular and never-uninteresting subject of . . . LOVE:

The wisest man the warl' e'er saw,
    He dearly lov'd the lasses, O.

*   *   *

What is life when wanting love?
    Night without a morning;
Love's the cloudless summer sun,
    Nature gay adorning.

*   *   *

Misery is like love; to speak its language truly, the author must have felt it.

*   *   *

The Burns Monument at Alloway village, near Ayr, Scotland, close to the poet's birthplace

Admirers from Moscow to Samoa and Tibet visit the little thatch-roofed cottage at Alloway village, near Ayr, where Burns was born on January 25, 175

The wit of Burns is heard at Burn Dinners round the world every January. The haggis (left) is piped-in at Dumfries Burns Club

Oh, gear will buy me rigs o' land,
   And gear will buy me sheep and kye*;
But the tender heart o' leesome luve
   The gowd* and siller canna buy.

(* kye=cows; gowd=gold)

*   *   *

If anything on earth deserves the name of rapture or transport, it is the feelings of green eighteen in the company of the mistress of his heart, when she repays him with an equal return of affection.

*   *   *

Burns loved the art of courtship. He had a friend, John Lees, in Tarbolton, Ayrshire, who accompanied him regularly in the evenings on visits to the homes of girls admired by the poet.

Lees would go in first and ask the girl if she would like to come out. Burns always waited by the door.

When Lees succeeded in bringing out another favourite lass of the poet, Burns would smile, put his arms round the girl, and say to his faithful aide:

Thank you, Jock. Now you can gang awa' hame!

*   *   *

The lovely Miss Eliza Burnett, younger of two daughters of Lord Monboddo, born in 1766, was a Scots maiden of outstanding beauty and grace. She entertained Burns at her father's famous suppers in Edinburgh.

Writing of her, Burns, an eager and ready admirer, said:

Fair Burnett strikes the adoring eye,
   Heav'n's beauties on my fancy shine;
I see the Sire of Love on high
   And own His work indeed divine!

*   *   *

Laughing at Death

The Scots have always shown a certain wit about death, and Robert Burns, a man who knew he would face death sooner than most, is no exception to the rule.

A friend of the poet, a melancholy type named Glendinning, took his life and was buried near Dumfries.
  A few days later Burns was seen kneeling by the grave-side and writing these lines on a piece of paper:

> Earth'd up here lies an imp o' hell,
>   Planted by Satan's dibble –
> Poor silly wretch, he's damn'd himsel'
>   To save the Lord the trouble.

*　　*　　*

In his poorer days, declining rapidly, Burns went out into the streets of Dumfries, shabby and disorderly. Meeting some close friends, he told them, sadly:

I am going to ruin as fast as I can; the best I can do, however, is to go consistently.

*　　*　　*

Writing to his lady friend Clarinda on 25th June 1794, Burns observed, not without humour:

When I am laid in my grave, I wish to be stretch'd at my full length, so that I may occupy every inch of ground I have a right to!

*　　*　　*

Robert Burns had warm memories of hospitality round Scotland, from both nobleman and peasant, as shown in these lines:

> When Death's dark stream I ferry o'er,
>   A time that surely shall come;
> In Heaven itself I'll ask no more
>   Than just a Highland welcome.

*   *   *

Even on his own death-bed, the wit and good humour of Burns shone through. According to Allan Cunningham, 'his wit never forsook him'. The poet talked to one of his fellow-volunteers as he stood by his bedside, his eyes wet, and, with the vestige of a smile, whispered:

John . . . John, don't let the Awkward Squad fire over me!

*   *   *

Burns was the author of this epitaph to William Hood senior, of Tarbolton, Ayrshire:

> Here Souter Hood in death does sleep;
> To Hell if he's gane* thither,
> Satan, gie him thy gear to keep;
> He'll haud* it weel thegither.

(* haud=hold; gane=gone)

*   *   *

Of James Grieve, Laird of Boghead, Tarbolton, the poet wrote these lines:

> Here lies Boghead amang the dead,
>   In hopes to get salvation;
> But if such as he, in Heav'n maybe,
>   Then welcome, hail! damnation.

*   *   *

Burns could turn out a neat epitaph, as in this one intended for the tombstone of a friend whom he did not regard as the wisest of men:

> Beneath this turf lies W—— G——
>   Nature thy loss bemoan;
> When thou wouldst make a fool again –
>   Thy choicest model's gone.

*   *   *

As he lay dying in Dumfries, Burns turned to his medical man, Dr Maxwell, the physician, and exclaimed:

What business has a physician to waste his time on me? I am a poor pigeon not worth plucking. Alas! I have not feathers enough upon me to carry me to my grave.

*   *   *

A blacksmith named Kilpatrick lived at a little place called Roads, near the Dumfriesshire village of Dalswinton. Burns had his home not far distant at the farm of Ellisland, and was one of his friends and customers.

The blacksmith challenged Burns to compose an epitaph to be placed on his tombstone.

Replied the poet, full of fun: 'That is a very easy matter. Just tell them to put on it:

> 'Below this sod lies drunken Roads
>   A man that ne'er lo'ed to drink water;
> The canty jill aye kittled his mill,
>   An' made his tongue gang clitter-clatter.'"

*   *   *

On Being Merry!

Robert Burns was a jolly Scot at heart, fond not only of the bonnie lasses but also of social get-togethers, carousals, and general revelry with wine, women and song. An evening of merriment was his idea of paradise, and his writings contain many references in wit to the pleasures of imbibing and being gay.

He sums up a carefree evening in a local inn in these two lines:
> Love blinks, Wit slaps, an' social Mirth
> Forgets there's care upon the earth.

*   *   *

In Tam O'Shanter *he says of drink:*
> Inspiring bold John Barleycorn!
>   What dangers thou can'st mak' us scorn!
> Wi' tippenny, we fear nae evil;
>   Wi' usquebae,* we'll face the devil!

(* usquebae=whisky)

*   *   *

And elsewhere:
> Freedom and Whisky gang thegither,
>   Tak aff your dram!

*   *   *

In Death and Dr Hornbrook:
I wasna fou but just had plenty.

*   *   *

In the song Contented Wi' Little, *Burns comments:*
My mirth and gude humour are coin in my pouch.

*   *   *

On being merry while you can, he advised:

> Catch the moments as they fly,
>   And use them as ye ought, man;
> Believe me, Happiness is shy,
>   And comes not aye when sought, man.

*   *   *

Burns could laugh at himself, even in merry and tipsy moments. Here is part of a letter he wrote to his Clarinda in June 1794:
You would laugh were you to see me where I am just now. Would to Heaven you were here to laugh with me, though I am afraid that crying would be our first employment.

Here am I set, a solitary hermit, in the solitary room of a solitary inn, with a solitary bottle of wine beside me – as grave and as stupid as an owl!

*   *   *

In another reference to the gaiety of the bottle, Burns wrote to a friend:
I have been in a dilemma – either to get drunk to fight my miseries, or to hang myself, to get rid of these miseries.

Like a prudent man . . . I have chosen the lesser of these two evils, and am very drunk at your service!

*   *   *

The witty Burns – contrary to the image many people have of him – had a real sense of enjoying life and revelling in his work, as these lines show:

> Some rhyme a neebor's name to lash;
>> Some rhyme (vain thought!) for needfu' cash;
> Some rhyme to court the country clash,
>> An' raise a din;
> For me, an aim I never fash*;
>> I rhyme for fun.

(* fash = worry about)

*   *   *

A doctor attending Burns in his last illness remonstrated with him about his fondness of drink, and assured him that 'the coat of your stomach is entirely gone.'

The merry poet retorted:

Ah, well, if that is the case, then I'll just go on drinking. If the coat is gone, it's no' worth the while to keep carrying about the waistcoat.

*   *   *

> To sum up all, be merry, I advise;
> And as we're merry, may we still be wise.

*   *   *

Say, you'll be merry, though you can't be rich!

*   *   *

> There's nane that's blest of human kind,
>> But the cheerful and the gay, man.

*   *   *

Burns is said to have scratched this line on a window in a Glasgow tavern:

Gie me with gay folly to live.

*   *   *

In a letter to Major Logan, he said:

> A blessing on the cheery gang
> Wha dearly like a jig or sang.

*   *   *

> Leeze me on Drink! it gies us mair
> Than either School or Colledge.

*   *   *

In the song The Rigs o' Barley:

I hae been merry drinking.

*   *   *

Writing to Mr Archibald Lawrie, of Edinburgh, Burns summed up his state of merry melancholy, thus:

Here I sit, in the Attic storey, alias the garret, with a friend on my right hand – a friend whose kindness I shall largely experience at the close of this line . . . a Friend, my dear Mr Lawrie, whose kindness often makes me blush; a Friend who has more of the milk of human kindness than all the human race put together, and what is highly to his honour, peculiarly a friend to the friendless as often as they come in his way; in short, sir, he is, without the least alloy, a universal Philanthropist; and his much beloved name is – A BOTTLE OF GOOD OLD PORT!

*   *   *

On another occasion, Burns remarked:
I suffer so much just now in this world for last night's joviality, that I shall escape Scot free for it, in the world to come!

*   *   *

My mirth an' good humour are coin in my pouch,
An' my freedom's my lairdship nae monarch dare touch.

*   *   *

Wit and Wisdom

Wisdom goes along with wit in many instances, and Robert Burns, poet and philosopher, wrote and talked much good common-sense in his lifetime.

The following is a selection of some of the choicest bits of Burns:

In Epistle to a Young Friend, *he wrote:*

> Conceal yoursel' as well's ye can
>   Frae critical dissection;
> But keek* thro' ev'ry other man
>   Wi' sharpen'd, sly inspection.

(* keek=look)

*   *   *

On another occasion, we find him saying:

There is a great degree of folly in talking unnecessarily about one's private affairs.

*   *   *

On the pleasures of life, Burns offers this oft-quoted adage:

> But pleasures are like poppies spread –
> You seize the flow'r, its bloom is shed;
> Or like the snow falls in the river –
>   A moment white, then melts for ever.

*   *   *

On the dangers of being too Puritanical:

> The rigid righteous is a fool,
> The rigid wise anither.

*   *   *

Too few people count their blessings, according to Burns. In a letter to Clarinda, he comments:

Nothing astonishes me more, when a little sickness clogs the wheels of life, than the thoughtless career we run in the hour of health.

*   *   *

On the subject of Misfortune, Burns wrote, in his Epistle to Davie:

> They gi'e the wit of age to youth,
> They let us ken* oursel'

(*ken=know)

*   *   *

On sycophants and flatterers:

How wretched is the man that hangs on by the favours of the great!

*   *   *

In a letter to Lady Glencairn:

I would much rather have it said that my profession borrowed credit from me than that I borrowed credit from my profession.

*   *   *

Burns had many a wise thought about the dangers of talking too much. Like this line of wit and wisdom, quoted in a letter to Mr James Smith:

'T is but poor consolation to tell the world when matters go wrong.

*   *   *

On the theory that one should 'neither a lender nor a borrower be', Burns said:

> I ha'e naething to lend –
>   I'll borrow from nobody.

*   *   *

In The Jolly Beggars, *he writes:*

> Life is all a variorum,
>   We regard not how it goes;
> Let them cant about decorum
>   Who have characters to lose.

*   *   *

In an Epistle to a Young Friend, *in 1786, Burns sums up the wisdom of not spilling secrets when he wrote:*

> But still keep something to yoursel'
>   Ye scarcely tell to ony.

*   *   *

The poet, of course, gave the world a pithy gem of wisdom in his poem To A Mouse. *In it, he wrote:*

> The best-laid schemes o' mice an' men
>   Gang aft a-gley,*
> And leave us nought byt grief and pain
>   For promised joy.

(* agley＝astray)

* * *

In A Bard's Epitaph, *he says:*

> Know prudent, cautious self-control
>   Is Wisdom's root.

* * *

On the folly of worrying over-much, Burns says, in his poem
The Twa Dogs:

> But human bodies are sic fools,
>   For a' their colleges and schools,
> That when nae real ills perplex them,
>   They mak' enow* themselves to vex them.

(* enow＝enough)

* * *

In Tam O' Shanter:

> Nae man can tether* time or tide.

(* tether＝hold up)

* * *

Of critics, Burns has this quite devastating description:

> Critics – appall'd, I venture on the name;
>   Those cut-throat bandits in the paths of fame.

* * *

The old red sandstone house in Dumfries, Scotland, where Burns died on July 21, 1796

Burns lovers pay tribute at this world-famed mausoleum, of Grecian temple design, in St. Michael's Churchyard, Dumfries, Scotland. The poet, his widow and five of their family are buried here

The poet's dislike for early rising is reflected in these lines:

Up in the mornin's no' for me,
Up in the morning early.

*   *   *

Burns was a tolerant man, and refused to be the type who would rashly condemn. He wrote:

I have often observed, in the course of my experience of human life, that every man – even the worst – has something of good about him.

*   *   *

In a letter to Mr Robert Airlie, Burns wrote:

'T is much to be a great character as a lawyer, but beyond comparison more to be a great character as a man.

*   *   *

Burns summed up his feelings on what is good and bad in this excerpt from a letter to Mrs Dunlop:

Whatever mitigates the woes, or increases the happiness, of others – this is my criterion of goodness; and whatever injures society at large, or any individual in it, this is my measure of iniquity.

*   *   *

Of a good wife, Burns gives this description:

The most placid, good-nature and sweetness of disposition; a warm heart, gratefully devoted with all its powers to love me; vigorous health and sprightly cheerfulness, set off to the best advantage by a more than commonly handsome figure; these, I think, in a woman, may make a good wife.

* * *

No man can say in what degree any other person, besides himself, can be, with strict justice, called – wicked.

* * *

Burns, always a man with human feeling, wrote thus of the person who makes an error in life:

> If ye ha'e made a step aside,
> Some hap-mistake o'er ta'en you,
> Yet, still keep up a decent pride,
> An' ne'er owre far demean you.
> Time comes wi' kind, oblivious shade
> An' daily darker sets it;
> An' if na-mae mistakes are made
> The warld soon forgets it.

* * *

On the same theme:

> Then gently scan your brother man,
> Still gentler sister woman;
> Tho' they may gang a kennin* wrang,
> To step aside is human.

(* kennin=a little bit)

* * *

Many writings and sayings of Burns reflect Robert Burns, the man of wit.

Here are a few:

Suspense is worse than disappointment.

*   *   *

Remorse is the most painful sentiment that can embitter the human bosom.

*   *   *

I trust I have too much pride for servility, and too little prudence for selfishness.

*   *   *

Novelty may attract the attention of mankind – for a while.

*   *   *

Every situation has its share of the cares and pains of life.

*   *   *

Fortune has so much forsaken me that she has taught me to live without her.

*   *   *

Hope is the cordial of the human heart.

*   *   *

It becomes a man of sense to think for himself.

*   *   *

Nature's gifts to all are free.

* * *

'T is well if we place an old idea in a new light.

* * *

I would always take it as a compliment to have it said that my heart ran before my head.

* * *

Every man has his virtues, and no man is without his failings.

* * *

The charms o' the mind, the langer they shine,
    The mair admiration they draw, man;
While peaches and cherries, and roses and lilies,
    They fade and they wither awa', man.

* * *

Do we not sometimes rather exchange faults than get rid of them?

* * *

Who knows them best, despise them most.
  (*A case of 'Familiarity breeding contempt', as it were*)

* * *

On a similar theme, Burns once said:
Far off fowls ha'e feathers fair.

*   *   *

Ambition is a meteor gleam,
   Fame an idle, restless dream.

*   *   *

Whether doing, suffering, or forbearing,
You may do miracles by persevering.

*   *   *

I despise the superstition of a fanatic, but I love the religion of a man.

*   *   *

On simplicity in life:
       Nae treasures, nor pleasures,
         Could make us happy lang;
       The heart's aye* the part aye
         That mak's us richt or wrang.
(* aye=always)

*   *   *

But facts are chiels that winna ding
   (*Facts are things you can't argue against*)

*   *   *

Age and Want. Oh! ill-match'd pair!

*   *   *

The man wha boasts o' warld's wealth,
Is often laird o' meikle* care.

(* meikle=much)

*   *   *

O wad some Power the giftie gi'e us,
To see oursel's as ithers see us!

*   *   *

Pass my faults, if you please, but spare my feelings.

*   *   *

And (g)if ye canna bite, ye may bark.

*   *   *

There is not a doubt but that health, talents, character,
decent competency, respectable friends, are real substantial
blessings.

*   *   *

To be just, and kind, and wise,
There solid self-enjoyment lies.

*   *   *

When my conscience tells me I am leaving something undone that I ought to do, it teases me eternally till I do it.

*　　*　　*

Burns said, once, that his own favourite quotation was:
>What proves the Hero truly great
>Is never, never to despair.

*　　*　　*

And again:
>Oh, what a canty* world were it,
>　Would pain, and care, and sickness spare it;
>And fortune favour worth and merit
>　As they deserve!

(* canty=cheerful, happy)

*　　*　　*

O' guid advisement comes nae ill
　(*Good advice never harmed anyone*)

*　　*　　*

Strange how apt we are to indulge prejudices in our judgements of one another.

*　　*　　*

Of all nonsense, religious nonsense is the most nonsensical.

*   *   *

The poet's deep-rooted hatred of people who toady to others is reflected in these lines:

I never . . . thought mankind capable of anything very generous; but the stateliness of the patricians of Edinburgh, and the servility of my plebeian brethren (who, perhaps, formerly eyed me askance), since I returned home, have nearly put me out of conceit altogether with my species.

*   *   *

Burns' rather sad outlook on man and mankind is shown in this advice to a youngster:

> Ye'll trythe world fu' soon, my lad,
>   And, Andrew dear, believe me,
> Ye'll find mankind an unco* squad
>   And muckle* they may grieve ye.

(* unco=strange; muckle=much)

*   *   *

In the same vein, his Epistle to a Young Friend *makes this comment:*

> But, och! mankind are unco weak,
>   And little to be trusted.

*   *   *

Again, Burns wrote:

> But, oh! what crowds in every land
> Are wretched and forlorn!
> Through weary life this lesson learn –
> That man was made to mourn.

*   *   *

Burns, in an Epitaph on a Friend, *commented philosophically:*

> If there's another world, he lives in bliss;
> If there is none, he made the best of this.

*   *   *

He gave this advice to a young friend:

> To catch Dame Fortune's golden smile,
> Assiduous wait upon her.

*   *   *

The poet's eternal optimism is seen in these two lines:

> The weary night o' care and grief
> May have a joyful morrow.

*   *   *

And he could laugh at himself, thus:

> O Life, though art a galling load,
> Along a rough, a weary road,
> To wretches such as I!

*   *   *

More sayings of wit and wisdom from the poet:
Ye are sae grave, nae doubt ye're wise.

*   *   *

How wisdom and folly meet, mix, and unite!

*　　　*　　　*

I live to-day as well's I may,
　　Regardless of to-morrow, O.

*　　　*　　　*

Beware a tongue that's smoothly hung.

*　　　*　　　*

My mirth and gude humour are coin in my pouch.

*　　　*　　　*

But pleasures are like poppies spread,
　　You seize the flower, its bloom is shed.

*　　　*　　　*

Burns, in a letter to his boyhood friend William Niven, in 1780, wrote at the age of 21:
A flatterer, next to a backbiter, is the most detestable character under the sun.

*　　　*　　　*

In a letter to Mr James Smith, of Linlithgow, written on 28th April 1788:
There is no understanding a man properly without knowing something of his previous ideas.

*　　　*　　　*

In a letter to John Francis Erskine:

Degenerate as human nature is said to be – and, in many instances, worthless and unprincipled it is – still there are bright examples to the contrary.

* * *

Writing to his friend Dr Blacklock, Burns commented:

Wha does the utmost that he can,
Will whiles* do mair*.

(* whiles=sometimes; mair=more)

* * *

In a letter to Mrs Dunlop:

Religion is surely a simple business, as it equally concerns the ignorant and the learned, the poor and the rich.

* * *

Burns was a sworn enemy of all who sought out the support of the powerful and lived on their strength. He once said:

How wretched is the man that hangs on by the favours of the great!

* * *

What insignificant sordid wretches are they, however chance may have loaded them with wealth, who go to their graves, to their magnificent mausoleums, with hardly the consciousness of having made one poor honest heart happy!

* * *

> Ambition is a meteor gleam,
> Fame an idle, restless dream.

*　　　*　　　*

In a letter to William Niven of Kirkoswald, Burns made this comment on Courage:

Courage I hold to be nothing else than a large portion of audacity . . . with a thoughtlessness of danger.

*　　　*　　　*

A certain Miss E. J. was a lady of Amazonian strength, a physical feature which prompted the bold Burns to coin this epigram:

> Should he escape the slaughter of thine Eyes,
>   Within thy strong Embrace he struggling dies.

*　　　*　　　*

Burns could always turn the tables against himself, and his tolerant sense of fun allowed him to joke about the perils of being a writer and a poet.

  Once, advising a friend not to take up the profession of a writer, he said:

The life of an Edinburgh Quill-driver (writer) at twopence a page is a life I know so well that I should be very sorry if any friend of mine should ever try it . . . A gentleman who prefers to live merely by the drudgery of his quill has before him a life of many sorrows.

*　　　*　　　*

In a letter to a friend in Alnwick, Northumberland, Burns wrote:

I have always held it a maxim in life, that in this bad world, those who truly wish us well are entitled to a pretty large share at least of our gratitude.

*   *   *

Burns disliked those who engaged in fighting and warfare, and then said prayers of thanks for winning. His scathing wit on this theme resulted in these lines:

> Ye hypocrites! are these your pranks?
>   To murder men and gie God thanks?
> Desist for shame! Proceed no further;
>   God won't accept your thanks for Murther.

*   *   *

The poet's image, worldwide, is one that covers a wide spectrum, but he is more often rated an advocate of drinking and carousing than an opponent of it. But he could show some wit in occasional condemnation of the imbibers, as in these lines from Tam O'Shanter:

> O Tam! hadst thou but been sae wise
> As ta'en thy ain wife Kate's advice!

*   *   *

Burns, in a letter to his friend Mr William Niven, merchant, of the town of Maybole, in Ayrshire:

Next to a backbiter, a flatterer is the most detestable character under the sun.

*   *   *

The poet, though often voted a rake and a man of loose morals by later generations, was nevertheless a staunch believer in God. Of times of trouble, he once said:

> But when on Life we're tempest-driv'n –
>   A conscience but a canker –
> A correspondence fix'd wi' Heav'n
>   Is sure a noble anchor.

*   *   *

Sensitive always to the danger and obnoxiousness of acquiring the fault of selfishness, Burns commented:

> If Self the wavering balance shake,
>   It's rarely right adjusted.

*   *   *

Burns had a healthy respect for fairness and law, and rounded on any who flouted it:

> The wretch that would a Tyrant own,
>   And the wretch, his true-sworn brother,
> Who would set the Mob above the Throne,
>   May they be damn'd together!

*   *   *

In a letter to Miss Chalmers, dated 19 December 1787, Burns said:

There are just two creatures that I would envy – a horse in his wild state traversing the forests of Asia, or an oyster on some of the desert shores of Europe. The one has not a wish without enjoyment; the other has neither wish nor fear.

*   *   *

Burns, unlike the wealthy merchants of his day, was averse to the tradition of fighting duels. Once, after quarrelling on a political matter, he wrote:

From the expressions Captain ———— made use of to me, had I had nobody's welfare to care for but my own, we should certainly have come, according to the manners of the world, to the necessity of murdering one another about the business. The words were such as, generally, I believe, end in a brace of pistols; but I am still pleased to think that I did not ruin the peace and welfare of a wife and a family of children in a drunken squabble.

*　　*　　*

On Honest Men

Throughout his life Burns was a staunch supporter of the ordinary man and woman, and a sworn opponent of anything that even faintly smacked of the false or, in modern parlance, 'phoney'.

> Ye see yon birkie* ca'd a lord,
>   Wha struts, and stares, an' a' that,
> Tho' hundreds worship at his word,
>   He's but a cuif* for a' that.

(* birkie=a conceited fellow; cuif=a fool)

*   *   *

> The rank is but the guinea stamp,
>   The man's the gowd* for a' that.

(* gowd=gold)

*   *   *

A man's a man for a' that.

*   *   *

On the subject of boasting, Burns had this to say:

What of Lords with whom you have supped,
  And of Dukes that you dined with yestreen!
A louse, sir, is still but a louse,
  Though it crawl on the locks of a queen.

*   *   *

*Burns expresses all the wit and humanity of honest men in his
famous Selkirk Grace, first said at the table of the Earl of Selkirk,
and quoted at banquets and dinners round the world:*

Some ha'e meat and canna eat,
  And some wad eat that want it,
But we ha'e meat, and we can eat,
  And sae the Lord be thanket.

*   *   *

What tho' on hamely fare we dine,
  A man's a man for a' that.

*   *   *

The honest heart that's free frae a'
  Intended fraud or guile,
However Fortune kick the ba'
  Has aye some cause to smile.

*   *   *

An honest man has nothing to fear.

*   *   *

The dignified and dignifying consciousness of an honest man, and the well-grounded trust in approving Heaven, are two most substantial sources of happiness.

* * *

Burns was taking a walk one day in the town of Leith when he met an old friend and stopped to talk with him.

  Next day, a rather uppity lady-friend of the poet asked him why he had thought fit to speak to so shabby-looking a person. To which Burns replied:

Madam, it was the man within I was talking to! Do you suppose it was the man's clothes I was addressing – his hat, his clothes, his boots?

* * *

And again:

Princes and Lords are but the breath of Kings,
An honest man's the noblest work of God.

* * *

Happy is our lot, indeed, when we meet with an honest merchant who is qualified to deal with us on our own terms – but that is a rarity.

* * *

I wouldn't be beholden to the noblest being ever God created, if he imagined me to be a rascal.

* * *

> The social, friendly, honest man,
>   Whate'er he be,
> 'T is he fulfils great Nature's plan,
>   And nane but he.

*   *   *

I have often courted the acquaintance of . . . blackguards. Though disgraced by follies, nay, sometimes stained with guilt, I have yet found among them, in not a few instances, some of the noblest virtues, magnanimity, generosity, disinterested friendship, and even modesty.

*   *   *

> The honest man, tho' e'er sae poor,
>   Is King of men for a' that.

*   *   *

On Contentment

A countryman who loved the simple life – fields, trees, animals, birds and flowers – Robert Burns was continually preaching the value of being content with your lot.

These lines from his writings on this subject have a certain degree of witty philosophy:

I hate the language of complaint.

*　　*　　*

It's no' in titles nor in rank;
　It's no' in wealth like Lon'on bank,
To purchase peace and rest.

*　　*　　*

Gi'e me ae spark o' Nature's fire,
　That's a' the learnin' I desire.

*　　*　　*

Hope not sunshine every hour,
　Fear not clouds will always lower.
Happiness is but a name,
　Make content and ease thy aim.

*　　*　　*

To make a happy fireside clime
　To weans and wife,
That's the true pathos and sublime
　Of human life.

*　　*　　*

All you who follow wealth and power
　With unremitting ardour, O,
The more in this you look for bliss,
　You leave your view the farther, O.

*　　*　　*

In his Epistle to Davie, *Burns wrote:*

If happiness ha'e not her seat
　And centre in the breast,
We may be wise, or rich, or great,
　But never can be blest.

*　　*　　*

A decent means of livelihood in the world, an approving
God, a peaceful conscience, and one firm trusty friend – can
anybody that has these be said to be unhappy?

*　　*　　*

This warld's wealth, when I think on
　Its pride, and a' the lave* o't –
Fie, fie on silly coward man,
　That he should be the slave o't.

(* lave=rest)

*　　*　　*

Wi' sma' to sell, and less to buy,
   Aboon distress, below envy,
Oh, who wad leave this humble state
   For a' the pride of a' the great?

*   *   *

Poverty and obscurity are only evils to him who can sit gravely down, and make repining comparison between his own situation and that of others.

*   *   *

I'll count my health my greatest wealth,
   Sae lang as I'll enjoy it.

*   *   *

Burns dearly loved to expound on the virtue of being independent and self-contained:
   I've little to spend, and naething to lend,
   But deevil a shilling I awe,* man.

(* awe = owe)

*   *   *

And, again, on the joy of the simple uncluttered life:
   As I was a-wandering ae morning in spring,
     I heard a merry ploughman sae sweetly to sing;
   And as he was singing, these words he did say,
     There's nae life like the ploughman's in the
       month o' sweet May.

*   *   *

I count my health my greatest wealth,
　　Sae lang as I'll enjoy it;
I'll fear nae scant, I'll bode nae want,
　　As lang's I get employment.

*　　　*　　　*

Content and luve bring peace and joy –
　　What mair hae queens upon a throne?

*　　　*　　　*

In a letter to Clarinda, he wrote:

My creed is pretty nearly expressed in the last clause of
Jamie Deans' grace, an honest weaver in Ayrshire. 'Lord,
grant that we may lead a gude life! for a gude life maks a
gude end.'

*　　　*　　　*

*Burns was one day at a wedding celebration when the country
lads and lasses engaged in the dance, and, as always, proved the
life and soul of the party. While he danced, there romped at his
heels his old faithful collie, the Luath of his* Twa Dogs.
　Said the poet:

Faith, I wish I could get ony o' the lasses to like me as weel
as my dog does.

*　　　*　　　*

*In a letter to a Maybole (Ayrshire) merchant, William Niven,
Burns wrote:*

I now see it improbable that I shall ever acquire riches, and
I am therefore endeavouring to gather a philosophical
contempt of enjoyment, so hard to gain and so easily lost.

*　　　*　　　*

And A' That

Burns is responsible for the wit of this epitaph to a schoolmaster from Kinross, in central Scotland, one William Michie:

> Here lies Willie Michie's banes;
>   O Satan, when ye tak' him,
> Gi'e him the schulin' o' your weans,
>   For clever de'ils he'll mak' em.

*　　　*　　　*

To a lady who suggested he was probably mixing too freely with friends and cronies in inns, Burns replied:

Madam, they would not thank me for my company if I did not drink with them. I must give them all a slice of my constitution.

*　　　*　　　*

Of his origin, Burns said:

My ancient, but ignoble blood, has crept through scoundrels ever since the flood.

*　　　*　　　*

This self-description is from Burns' Commonplace Book:

Robert Burness; a man who had little art in making money, and still less in keeping it; but was, however, a man of some sense, a great deal of honesty, and unbounded goodwill to every creature, rational and irrational.

*　　*　　*

Burns was invited, during his time as an Excise-man, to a special social occasion. He replied thus, in verse:

> The King's most humble servant, I
> 　Can scarcely spare a minute;
> But I am yours at dinner-time,
> 　Or else the devil's in it.

*　　*　　*

Of his eldest boy, he wrote in a letter:

I intend breeding him up for the Church; and, from an innate dexterity in secret Mischief which he possesses, and a certain hypocritical gravity as he looks on the consequences, I have no small hopes of him in the sacerdotal line.

*　　*　　*

The witty thrust in favour of ordinary people is seen in these lines:

> Who will not sing 'God Save the King'
> 　Shall hang as high's the steeple,
> But while we sing 'God Save the King',
> 　We'll ne'er forget the People.

*　　*　　*

In Epistle to a Young Friend, *the poet makes this comment on the wisdom of living honourably:*

> The fear o' Hell's a hangman's whip,
>   To haud the wretch in order;
> But where ye feel your Honor grip,
>   Let that ay be your border.

*   *   *

Burns' description of the West Highlands of Scotland:

Where savage streams tumble over savage mountains, thinly overspread with savage flocks, which starvingly support as savage inhabitants.

*   *   *

In March 1784, Burns said:

Let any of the strictest character for regularity of conduct among us, examine impartially how many vices he has never been guilty of, not from any care or vigilance, but for want of opportunity, or some accidental circumstance intervening; how many of the weaknesses of mankind he has escaped, because he was out of the line of such temptation.

*   *   *

In a letter to a friend, he wrote:

I scorn the affectation of seeming modesty to cover self-conceit. That I have some merit, I do not deny; but I see, with frequent wringings of heart, that the novelty of my character, and the honest national prejudice of my countrymen, have borne me to a height altogether untenable to my abilities.

*   *   *

75

One day Burns' farmer employer and a friend, Mr Johnstone, were passing through a stable arch where Burns, as a stable-boy, was sweeping out the stable-door. The two men thought they would make fun of the poet lad, and Johnstone said:

> 'You silly loon, lay down your broom
> Till Johnstone he pass by.'

To which Burns, throwing his broom to the other side, retorted:

> Just like an ass, let Johnstone pass
> Between my broom and I.

*   *   *

On another occasion, when two farmers were passing him and thought to have some fun at Burns' expense, one said 'Boo' as they went by.

Quick as a flash, the young poet answered:

> There's Mr Scott and Mr Boyd
>   Of grace and manners they are void;
> Just like the bull amang the kye*
>   They say 'Boo' at folk when they gae by.

(* kye=cows)

*   *   *

In a letter to Mrs Chalmers, Burns wrote:

The question is not at what door of fortune's palace we shall enter in, but what door does she open to us.

*   *   *

In another letter, the poet offers these lines of sharp observation:

Of the many problems in the nature of that wonderful creature, man, this is one of the most extraordinary – that he should go on from day to day, from week to week, from month to month, or perhaps from year to year, suffering a hundred times more in an hour from the important consciousness of neglecting what he ought to do, than the very doing of it would cost him.

*   *   *

Burns felt the injustices of life deeply, as in these lines:

    Oh, why has worth so short a date,
      While villains ripen grey with time?

*   *   *

The poet employs the wit of invective in this earthy advice to take a look at one's self:

    How daur ye ca' me 'Howlet-faced'?*
      Ye blear-eyed, wither'd spectre!
    Ye only spied the keekin'-glass*
      An' there ye saw your picture.

(* Howlet-faced=having face like an owl; keekin'-glass= mirror)

*   *   *

In his Address to the Unco Guid, *Burns hit out at the ultra-pious in the community:*

    O ye wha are sae guid yoursel',
      Sae pious and sae holy,
    Ye've nought to do but mark and tell
      Your neebour's fau'ts and folly!

*   *   *

Of his start in writing, Burns said:

I am going to commence poet in print, and to-morrow my works go to the press. I expect it will be a volume of about two hundred pages.

It is just the last foolish action I intend to do; and then turn a wise man as fast as possible.

*　　*　　*

There is a dash of wit in Burns' account of his becoming famous:

For my own affairs, I am in a fair way of becoming as eminent as Thomas a Kempis or John Bunyan; and you may expect henceforth to see my birthday inserted among the wonderful events, in the Poor Robin's and Aberdeen Almanacks, along with the Black Monday and the Battle of Bothwell Bridge.

*　　*　　*

Who else but a man of offbeat wit and happy humour would have dreamt of addressing a poem to – a Scotch haggis?

> Fair fa' your honest sonsie* face,
>   Great chieftain o' the puddin'-race!
> Aboon them a' ye tak' your place,
>   Painch,* tripe, or thairm:*
> Weel are ye worthy o' a grace
>   As lang's my arm.

(* sonsie＝jolly; Painch＝paunch; thairm＝gut)

*　　*　　*

Burns has this succinct summing-up of the human race:

Lord! What is man? What a bustling little bundle of passions, appetites, ideas and fancies!

*　　*　　*

And this comment on young people:

Young men may be divided into two classes . . . the grave and the merry.

The grave . . . are goaded on by the love of money; the merry are the men of pleasure of all denominations, the jovial lads who have too much fire and spirit to have any settled rule of action.

*　　　*　　　*

Burns was not shy at voicing his views on religion and the Church, but was always able to smile at the reaction he called forth:

Polemical divinity about this time (1787) was putting the country half-mad, and I, ambitious of shining in conversation parties on Sundays and at funerals, used to puzzle Calvinism with so much heat and indiscretion, that I raised a hue-and-cry of heresy against me, which has not ceased to this hour.

*　　　*　　　*

The poet was a sworn enemy of hypocrites, humbug and those who refused anyone freedom, as these telling lines prove:

> Here's freedom to him that wad read,
>> Here's freedom to him that wad write!
> There's nane ever fear'd that the truth
>> should be heard
> But they wham the truth wad indite.

*　　　*　　　*

Another witty comment on life:

The world is so busied with selfish pursuits – ambition, vanity, interest or pleasure – that very few think it worth

THE WIT OF ROBERT BURNS

their while to make any observation on what passes around them, except where that observation is a sucker, or branch, of the darling plant they are rearing in their fancy.

*　　*　　*

Burns has left us a fair number of shrewd and witty comments on life in general:

Life is a fairy scene; almost all that deserves the name of enjoyment and pleasure is only a charming delusion; and in comes repining age, in all the gravity of hoary wisdom, and wretchedly chases away the bewitching phantom.

*　　*　　*

If to know one's errors were a probability of mending them, I stand a fair chance.

*　　*　　*

Where is firmness of mind shown but in exertion?

*　　*　　*

There is nothing in the whole frame of man which seems to be so unaccountable as that thing called conscience.

*　　*　　*

My life reminds me of a ruined temple; what strength, what proportion in some parts! What unsightly gaps, what prostrate ruin in others!

*　　*　　*

Even in his most outspoken moments – and they were many – Burns could reveal a clever turn of phrase; as in this excerpt from a letter to Mrs Dunlop in Edinburgh:

Poets, much my superiors, have so flattered those who possessed the adventitious qualities of wealth and power that I am determined to flatter no created being, either in prose or verse, so help me God. I set as little by kings, lords, clergy, critics, etc. as all these respectable Gentry do by my Bardship.

* * *

To an Edinburgh artist who, in Burns' view, was over-taxing his talents, the poet sent these naughty lines:

> You shouldna paint at angels mair,
>   But try and paint the devil.
> To paint an Angel's kittle* wark,
>   Wi' Nick, there's little danger:
> Ye'll easy draw a long-kent face,
>   But no sae weel a stranger.

(* kittle=ticklish)

* * *

In his poem My Love She's But A Lassie Yet!, *Burns tilts amusingly at the clergy:*

> The minister kiss'd the fiddler's wife,
>   An' couldna preach for thinkin' o't!

* * *

On a visit to the pretty health resort of Moffat, in the Dumfriesshire hills, Burns saw two ladies ride past – one tall and pretty, the other almost the 'bonnie wee thing' of his poems.

A friend asked him why God had made Miss Davies so tiny while her companion was so large. He replied in verse:

>Ask why God made the gem so small,
>   And why so huge the granite;
>Because God meant mankind should set
>   The higher value on it.

*   *   *

Burns always showed a neat turn of wit whenever Scotland's national dish, the haggis, came under review:

>Ye Powr's wha mak' mankind your care
>And dish them out their bill o' fare,
>Auld Scotland wants nae skinking ware*
>   That jaups in luggies;*
>But if ye wish her grateful' prayer,
>   Gie her a Haggis!

(* skinking ware=thin stuff; jaups in luggies=splashes in bowls)

*   *   *

Always a sworn enemy of empty pomp and pageantry, insincerity and false airs, the poet was biting in his condemnation of the artificial, as in this extract from The Cotter's Saturday Night:

>Compar'd with this, how poor Religion's pride,
>   In all the pomp of method, and of art;
>When men display to congregations wide
>   Devotion's ev'ry grace, except the heart!

*   *   *

Burns, always sympathetic to the ordinary man and woman-in-the-street, loved to use his humorous pen in tilting at authority. The Government Exciseman seeking the tax and duty-evaders, was often his target:

>We'll mak' our maut* and we'll brew our drink,
>   We'll laugh, sing and rejoice, man!
>And monie braw thanks to the meikle* black Deil
>   That danc'd awa' wi' th' Exciseman.

>There's threesome reels, there's foursome reels,
>   There's hornpipes and strathspeys, man,
>But the ae best dance e'er cam' to the Land
>   Was 'The Deil's awa' wi' th' Exciseman.'

(* maut=malt; meikle=big)

*   *   *

Sometimes the wit of Burns could be devastating, as when he turned on poets more learned than himself:

>There's ither poets, much your betters,
>Far seen in Greek, deep men o' letters,
>Hae thought they had ensur'd their debtors,
>   A' future ages;
>Now moths deform, in shapeless tatters,
>   Their unknown pages.

*   *   *

Every situation has its share of the cares and pains of life.

*   *   *

> On peace an' rest, my min' was bent,
> And, fool I was, I married.

*   *   *

Misfortunes are not always sent to try us; they can often add a touch of good humour and wit to everyday living, according to the poet:

> They gie the wit of age to youth;
>   They let us ken* oursel;
> They make us see the naked truth –
>   The real guid* and the ill;
> Tho' losses an' crosses
>   Be lessons right severe,
> There's wit there, ye'll get there,
>   Ye'll find nae other where.

(* ken=know; guid=good)

*   *   *

Robert Burns used a picturesque turn of wit to attack the conceited types he encountered among the pseudo-academics of his day:

> A set o' dull, conceited hashes*
> Confuse their brains in college-classes!
> They gang in stirks,* and come out asses,
>   Plain truth to speak;
> An' syne they think to climb Parnassus
>   By dint o' Greek!

(* hashes=fellows; gang in stirks=go in as steers)

*   *   *

The philosophy of Burns was spiced throughout with gentle humour and satiric wit. He took pride in being humble and poor, advocated that a person should make the best of misfortunes, and accepted the state of the world as being far from perfect:

> It's hardly in a body's pow'r,
> To keep, at times, frae being sour,
>   To see how things are shar'd;
> How best o' chiels* are whyles* in want,
> While coofs* on countless thousands rant,
>   And ken na how to ware't;
> But Davie, lad, ne'er fash* your head,
>   Tho' we hae little gear;*
> We're fit to win our daily bread,
> As lang's we're hale* and fier.*

(* chiels=men; whyles=sometimes; coofs=fools; fash= trouble; gear=wealth; hale=healthy; fier=vigorous)

*   *   *

Whatever other qualities he prized, Burns must have been happy that he had the wit and good sense always to laugh at himself, and never to take himself too seriously. In Second Epistle to Davie, *he writes of his own work and sums it up in five words:*

My puir, silly, rhymin' clatter!

*   *   *

In a letter to Mr Cruikshank, Burns quipped on the subject of Apologies:

Apologies for not writing are frequently like apologies for not singing – the apology is better than the song.

*   *   *

Although nearly always in a state of poverty, Burns could still laugh at life and the humour of being short of cash:

> When sometimes by my labour
> I earn a little money, O,
> Some unforeseen misfortune
> Comes generally upon me, O.

* * *

In a letter in December 1793, Burns wrote to Mr John McMurdo of Drumlanrig:

It is said that we take the greatest liberties with our greatest friends, and I pay myself a very high compliment in the manner in which I am going to apply the remark. I have owed you money longer than ever I owed it to any man.

* * *

Burns could be wicked in his wit about the ladies, as shown by this verse which he penned, marked Pinned to a Lady's Coach:

> If you rattle along like your Mistress's tongue,
> Your speed with out-rival the dart;
> But, a fly for your load, you'll break down
>   on the road
> If your stuff be as rotten's her heart.

* * *

Burns brought some of his wit to the subject of matrimony:

I often think it is owing to lucky chance more than to good management that there are not more unhappy marriages than usually are.

* * *

In a letter to Clarinda, he wrote:

Happy is our lot, indeed, when we meet with an honest merchant who is qualified to deal with us on our own terms; but that is a rarity.

*   *   *

Again:

Remorse is the most painful sentiment that can embitter the human bosom.

*   *   *

Misery is like love. To speak its language truly, the author must have felt it.

*   *   *

In a letter to Mrs Dunlop:

A mathematician without religion is a probable character; an irreligious poet is a monster.

*   *   *

As all students of his poems know, Robert Burns was not the man who could stand fools easily.

In 1794 a Mr Swan was elected a Bailie of the town of Dumfries, and a Mr John McMurdo was voted Provost. There was a celebration to mark their success, at which Burns the poet, asked to write some lines, came out with this (later he proved himself a bit of a prophet, the same Bailie being ousted from office):

> Baillie, Swan, Baillie Swan,
>   Let you do what you can,
> God ha' mercy on honest Dumfries,
>   But, e'er the year's done,
> Good Lord! Provost John
>   Will find that his *Swans* are but *Geese.*

*   *   *

Writing in September 1792 to Mrs Dunlop, Burns wryly commented:

I am not equal to the task of rearing girls. Besides, I am too poor. A girl should always have a fortune.

*　　*　　*

When a public library was opened in Dumfries, Burns, in September 1793, presented four books to it – Humphrey Clinker, Julia de Roubigne, Knox's History of the Reformation, *and* De Lolme on the British Constitution.

In the fly-leaf of the last-named, Burns wrote this inscription: Mr Burns presents this book to the Library and begs they will take it as a creed of British liberty – until they find a better.

*　　*　　*

Burns' love of humanity and friendliness was aimed at making the world a better place for all to live in:

God knows I'm no saint, but if I could – and I think I do it as far as I am able – I would wipe all tears from all eyes.

*　　*　　*

Burns went one day to dinner at the Brownhill Inn where the landlord was, oddly enough, named Bacon, and the principal dish on the menu happened to be – bacon!

When the landlord retired to replenish the whisky, an English stranger asked the poet to give evidence that he really was the poet Burns. The latter immediately wrote some verse, then stood up and proclaimed:

At Brownhill we always get dainty good cheer,
   And plenty of bacon each day in the year;
We've all things that's nice and mostly in season;
   But why always *Bacon* – come give me the reason?

*   *   *

In Edinburgh Burns became friendly with William Creech, bookseller and Lord Provost of the city from 1811 to 1813. His bookshop in the Luckenbooths attracted the writing types of the day, and his house in Craig's Close was famous for morning literary meetings at breakfast time, known to all and sundry as 'Creech's Levees.'

   On the occasion of Creech having to go to London on business, Burns addressed to him a poetical epistle, sly suggesting that nobody else offered a meeting-place:

    Now worthy Gregory's Latin face,
       Tytler's and Greenfield's modest grace;
    Mackenzie, Stewart, such a brace
       As Rome ne'er saw;
    They a' maun meet some ither place,
       Willie's awa!

*   *   *

A friend of Burns bought a Bible and paid a small fortune to have it bound most elegantly. He asked the poet to write something on the blank leaf.

   Burns wrote:

    Free thro' the leaves ye maggots make your windings,
    But for the Owner's sake, Oh spare the Bindings!

*   *   *

For Auld Lang Syne

Through his thoughts and writings, the theme of friendship between people is paramount. Burns wanted everyone to be friendly – nations, neighbours, rich and poor, high and low. He preached universal brotherhood.

For auld lang syne, my dear,
   For auld lang syne,
We'll tak' a cup o' kindness yet,
   For auld lang syne.

*   *   *

For a' that, and a' that,
   It's comin' yet for a' that,
That Man to Man, the world o'er,
   Shall brithers be for a' that!

*   *   *

Man's inhumanity to man,
   Makes countless thousands mourn.

*   *   *

In Epistle to Davie, *he said:*
   The heart aye's the part aye,
     That makes us right or wrang.

If Burns had been with us today, he would have been a most prolific writer of observations and witty comments in those Visitors' Books which are still a feature of the lobbies of hotels and guest-houses.

After a night of revelry with companions, he once took a walk over the Pentland Hills near Edinburgh until dawn, and returned to breakfast at the home of their hostess, Mrs David Wilson, of Roslin, near Edinburgh.

She served up a most appetising breakfast.

Burns, in gratitude, composed some lines, as was his habit, and scribbled them on the reverse side of a wooden platter:

> My blessings on you, honest wife,
> I ne'er was here before,
> You've walth i' gear for spoon and knife;
> Heart could not wish for more.
>
> Heaven keep you clear of sturt and strife,
> Till far ayont four-score;
> And by the Lord o' death and life,
> I'll ne'er gae by your door.

*　　　*　　　*

This story (told by Fred J. Belford, a Burns scholar and enthusiast) concerns a typical Burns Supper, the type where speakers with little Scottish blood and a lack of knowledge of the Scottish tongue, speak out with synthetic eloquence about the poet from Alloway.

Proposing the 'Immortal Memory' at a Scots Society Burns Supper in England, Mr Belford listened in awe as a very English Caledonian Society chairman proceeded to address the Haggis:

> Fair *fae* your honest, sonsy face,
> Great Chieftain of the *pudding* race,
> Aboon them *all* you *take* your place,
>   Painch, tripe or thairm;
> *Well* are *you worthy* of a grace
> As lang's my *fit*.

*　　　*　　　*

In a letter to Clarinda, Robert Burns revealed some of his inner-most feelings with a goodly quota of witty phrase:

I don't know if you have a just idea of my character, but I wish you to see me as I am. I am, as most people of my trade are, a strange will-o'-wisp being; the victim too frequently of much imprudence and many follies.

My great constituent elements are Pride and Passion. The first I have endeavoured to humanise into integrity and honour, the last makes me a Devotee in the warmest degree of enthusiasm in Love, Religion or Friendship

*   *   *

Acknowledgements

The wit and humour of Robert Burns is extensive, and full credit is given to the ploughman poet himself for providing the compiler with so many varied aspects of his humour. Burns himself might have been the last person to admit of his own witty streak, but it cannot now be denied, and full acknowledgement must go to the humble poet and versifier from south-west Scotland for the excerpts used in this compilation.

Thanks are also due to the staff of the Mitchell Library, Glasgow, for facilities to study their excellent collection of Burnsiana, and to Scots and English in many towns and villages, including Margaret Graham, of Beeswing, Dumfries, and James McPhail, of Dumfries, for rallying round with stories, anecdotes and epigrams from the life of Burns.